THE ELDER

CHARACTER AND DUTIES

William Caldwell Macdonald

SAINT ANDREW PRESS

Edinburgh

First published in 1958 by
STIRLING TRACT ENTERPRISE

First revised edition published in 1982
Second revision in 1991 by
SAINT ANDREW PRESS
121 George Street, Edinburgh EH2 4YN

Reprinted 1992, 1996, 1999, 2004

ISBN 0 7152 0658 3

Printed and bound by Mackay & Inglis Ltd, Glasgow

Foreword

THE chapters of this little book were originally given at a conference for Church of Scotland elders and office-bearers; but the problems dealt with are common to the office-bearers of every Church. Every minister in Scotland knows the difficulty of finding the right individuals to take up positions of responsibility. Much of the trouble in the world today arises from the fact that the wrong people are in the wrong jobs—too many round pegs in square holes. Similarly a lot of the trouble in the Christian Church arises from the fact that there are some people trying to do church work who may be cultured, charming people, but they are secular in outlook and worldly at heart. They have not been changed by Christ. They may have become members of the Church simply because they wanted to get married or have a child baptized. They then may have been invited to take up positions of responsibility.

All down the centuries, from the days of Christ to our own, these are the people who cause most trouble in the Church. To try to live the Christian life *without Christ* is impossible. To attempt any work for Christ and his Church before Christ has changed us is simply heading for disaster. We will not only hurt ourselves; we shall hurt others and bring discredit on the Church of Christ. In the following chapters we shall discuss the kind of person who can serve Christ and his Church and we shall look at some of the problems which all Christians are facing today.

Part I

The Elder in the Session

ONE day a minister called to see a businessman whom he was anxious to ordain as an elder: a man of fine character, with a gracious, kind spirit, in every way suited to hold this high office. But the man had doubts, hesitations, even theological difficulties. The minister did his best to remove these, and after one or two interviews, he managed to persuade the man. Later on, at an impressive church service, he had the joy of ordaining him to the office of the eldership.

From time to time, congregations all over the country are faced with the problem of finding new elders; and sometimes, for one reason or another, those most fitted for the office hold back. They have doubts. When approached by their minister they may ask, 'What does becoming an elder involve?' Let us now look at that question.

But first, before dealing with practical matters, let us glance briefly at the history of the eldership.

The Origin of the Eldership

The eldership is the most ancient of all offices within the Church, going back to the Old Testament. The Jews had elders, and they traced their origin to the occasion when Moses, in the journey to the Promised Land, appointed seventy men to help him in the task of controlling and caring for the people. Moses was feeling the burden of leadership and, being a deeply religious man, he brought the matter to God in the intimacy of prayer: 'How have I displeased the Lord that I am burdened with the care of this whole people? Am I their mother? Have I brought them into the world, and am I called upon to carry them in my bosom, like a nurse with her babies, to the land promised by thee on oath to their fathers? ... This whole people is a burden too heavy for me' (Numbers 11:12, 14, NEB).

God answered his prayer by telling him to appoint seventy men to help him in this task. He promised that when the men were appointed, the Spirit of God would fill their hearts—the same Spirit that rested on Moses. 'I will come down and speak with you there. I will take back part of that same spirit which has been conferred on you and confer it on them, and they will share with you the burden of taking care for the people; then you will not have to bear it alone.'

And that is exactly what happened. The seventy were appointed, and the Spirit of God came upon them and they started to prophesy. But it so happened that two of them were not in the tabernacle at the time; they were in the camp. They too started to prophesy. A young man ran to tell Moses. It so happened that at that moment Joshua, who was to succeed Moses in the leadership of the people, was nearby; and he said, 'My lord Moses, forbid them'. But Moses said to him, 'Are you jealous on my account? I wish that all the Lord's people were prophets and that the Lord would confer his spirit on them all!'

Moses did not want a monopoly of the Spirit for himself or the seventy. He wanted it for everybody. That was the democratic basis on which the eldership was founded, and that democratic character has always marked the office of the eldership.

When we pass from the Old to the New Testament, we find that in the time of Jesus every synagogue had its elders. These men were the real leaders of the Jewish community. They presided over the worship of the synagogue; they administered discipline when necessary; they settled all kinds of disputes which other nations would have settled in courts of law. Among the Jews, the elders were respected men who kept a fatherly eye on the spiritual and material affairs of every Jewish community.

After the resurrection of Jesus, when the Church came into being, the office of the elder was recognized in the early Church. It was adopted with many other features of the synagogue. Elders were appointed in all the churches. In the Book of Acts we are told that after their first missionary tour, Paul and Barnabas appointed elders in the churches they had founded: 'And when they had ordained them elders in every church, and had prayed with fasting, they commended them to the Lord, on whom they believed' (Acts 14:23).

The Roman Catholic Church

When we pass from the New Testament into the early years of Christianity, and the Church begins to take the shape of the Roman Church, we find that the office of the layman is pushed into the background, while the office of priest is magnified.

I was once asked to write a little booklet explaining the differences between the Church of Scotland and the Roman Catholic Church, published under the title *How Protestant is*

Scotland? I arranged an interview with a Roman Catholic priest to get some background information about the place of the layman in the Church, and I asked him if the Catholic Church had a body of people equivalent to the Church of Scotland Session. He told me that there was no such body of people. What about a Session Clerk? No. Or a Treasurer? No. So who looks after the money? The priest told me how he gathers the money together on Sunday night and takes it to the bank on the Monday morning. And no account of this is given to the congregation.

In other words, the Roman Catholic Church is an entirely priest-governed Church and the layman has little say in the control and direction of Church affairs.

Elders appear in Scotland

When the Reformation came to Scotland, John Knox speedily revived the office of the eldership; elders appeared in Scotland just before 1560. In certain towns, like Edinburgh and Dundee, Protestants began to meet for prayer and scripture study. They sought, in the words of John Knox, *'to have the face of a Kirk amanges us and open crimes to be punished without respect of persone. For this purpose by common election war elders appointed to whom the hole brethren promise obedience; for at that time we had not public ministers of the work'.* The *First Book of Discipline* assumes the existence of elders and states that they shall be *'of the best knowledge in God's word, of cleanest life, faithful and of most honest conversation that may be found in the Church'.* They are to be nominated to the congregation, and if the nature of their lifestyle and doctrine approved of, elected by it. Election is to be annually, *'lest by long continuance in office men presume upon the liberty of the Church'*. But an elder who had proved his fitness was eligible for re-election.

And so by 1560 the elders appeared in Scotland, and it is impossible to tell what the eldership has meant to our country during the last 400 years? Who can estimate its far-reaching influence upon the character of our people? Think of the centuries of education in public and religious responsibility represented in Scotland by the office of the elder: all manner of men and, more recently, women, sitting side by side in counsel, standing side by side in prayer, visiting the homes of people in health and sickness, distributing the communion cards, bearing the bread and wine from the communion table to renew the strength of those who wait upon the Lord. Who can estimate the influence of all this? Perhaps it is not too much to say that the eldership of the Scottish Church has been the backbone of the Scottish people.

Duties of the Eldership

Having discussed the *history* of the office of the elder, let us now pass on to say something about the *duties*. In a Report on Relations between Anglican and Presbyterian Churches, the following paragraph appears:

> In each parish there is a Kirk Session which consists of the minister and lay elders, the minister being the Moderator of the Session, and usually a senior elder being Session Clerk. The quorum is three, the Moderator and two elders; but in large congregations the number of elders may rise to nearly a hundred. The present average throughout the Church is approximately twenty elders per parish minister. It rests with each Session to determine the number of elders required for the particular congregation. These

may be selected by the congregation or by the Session itself. The names are publicly announced to the congregation by intimation on two Sundays, and an opportunity is given to state objections. If none are stated or substantiated, those selected are then at a public service set apart to the eldership, and inducted to office in the particular congregation.

The elder's duties are discharged partly in the Kirk Session, and partly as an individual outside it. As a member of Session, the elder has certain responsibilities. The Session is responsible for the due and reverent observance of the sacraments—Baptism and the Lord's Supper—and for the regulation of the admission and the general conduct of members of the congregation. It is responsible for the education of the young, and for all youth organizations: like Sunday School, Bible Class and Youth Fellowship. The Session is also responsible for any social or recreational activity which takes place within church buildings. It arranges for any necessary congregational meetings and authorizes the use of the church or hall for special services and other occasions. It receives an annual report from the local branch of the Woman's Guild. It is responsible for the Home Mission work of the congregation, which includes Church extension; and also for the interest of the congregation in the work of the Church overseas. The care of the indigent member, the nature and conduct of public worship, and the consideration of matters of social responsibility and evangelical outreach belong to the Session. The Session is also responsible for the appointment of the organist and the Church Officer.

Needless to say, some of these duties are delegated. The minister is charged with the conduct of public worship and is given power to arrange and modify it. Most churches have either a Board of Management or Deacons' Court who look after the financial side of church work and fabric.

But it is a good thing for the Session to keep in touch with all the different organizations of the church. In some congregations the Session appoints two of their number to visit all the congregational organizations—Sunday School, Bible Class, Youth Fellowship, Woman's Guild, choir and so on—and to report accordingly. That involves a great deal of work for two individuals, so in some Sessions one elder is appointed to each organization—one to the Bible Class, one to the Sunday School, another to the choir and so on. These individuals are usually appointed at the September meeting of the Session, and they report at the December meeting. Their visit is usually welcomed by the different organizations, who feel that the Session is actively interested; and, of course, should any trouble arise anywhere, the Session is better informed to deal with it. The visiting elders must employ discretion and avoid the tactless approach of one man I knew who, when visiting a certain Sunday School, began his address by saying, *'Well, what a difference from the days when I was a boy attending Sunday School. In those days the hall was crowded to overflowing!!!'*

The individual elder, therefore, is a member of the Session, and the Session has a certain amount of power and responsibility. The minister, meanwhile, is under the jurisdiction of the Presbytery, not the Session; but a wise minister will be one who works well with the elders, for in our Presbyterian Church a minister is greatly dependent on the Session. The elders, by loyalty and co-operation, can do much to help their minister; but they can do just as much to hinder him or her as well. For, after all, minister and elders cannot always see eye to eye on everything. It would be strange if they did. We are all entitled to our own point of view and the freedom to express it. That is the democratic nature of the Session and the eldership. Even in the Apostolic Church there were differences of opinion among the elders; but we are told they were of 'one heart and one soul'—that is what matters. Without such unity in the Session there can be no blessing on any Church.

Duties in more Detail

Let us now deal with the duties of the eldership in more detail. It is sometimes said that they are threefold: to attend meetings of Session, to look after an elder's district, and to assist with the distribution of the bread and wine on a Communion Sunday. Above all, in all things affecting the welfare of the congregation, the elder should be an example to others.

One of the elder's first duties is to attend church regularly on Sunday. This is important not only for the sake of his (or her) own spiritual life, but for the encouragement which his presence gives both to the minister and to fellow-members, and especially to the young people of the congregation. It cannot be expected that a congregation will prosper if its elders are absent from the services without due cause. If we want our young people to come to church regularly, those of us who are older must show a good example; and in churches where there are two services, when the Session asks the minister to preach in the evening as well as the morning, it is always encouraging to see some of the elders present at the evening service. People do ask, 'Why are so few elders present at the evening service?' Perhaps the elders themselves do not realize how much their presence can encourage their minister and fellow worshippers.

The elder is expected to be present on Communion Sunday and to help with the distribution of the bread and wine; this is something which, in all our churches, is done with great reverence. We ministers owe much to our elders for the help they give us on a Communion Sunday, and for the quiet, reverent way in which the Communion service is carried out. In large congregations, where thirty or forty elders may be engaged in a Communion service, this means a great deal of work for one of the elders who has to make the arrangements and give the other elders their duties. This work is of great importance, for the spiritual side of a Communion service is to some extent dependent on the mechanical side; and the atmosphere of a Communion service can be so easily wrecked, just like the atmosphere of an ordinary service.

Writing in *The British Weekly*, William Barclay once related the following incident:

> A short time ago I was preaching in a certain church. The sermon had been preached; the service was coming to its close; and there was an atmosphere in the little congregation in which Jesus Christ was very near. We were singing the last hymn: we had come to the lines—*Thou, O Christ, art all I want; More than all in Thee I find*—and there were people there who were singing it with all their hearts; and then, just at these very lines, an office-bearer shut his hymnbook, took off his spectacles, snapped them into his case, and stumped down the aisle, no doubt importantly to take his place at the door as the people went out—and the atmosphere was wrecked.

And then William Barclay added this paragraph:

I know that someone must wait at a service to see that latecomers get in, and I know that certain things must be done. But I also know this—that Church office-bearers did not receive their office that they might have an irreverent freedom which others must not share, but that they should be an example of reverence to the rest of the congregation. It is a tragic thing that office-bearers of the Church and officials of the Church often show the least reverence during the services and meetings of the Church, and are most guilty of wrecking the atmosphere of worship which should be there.

This is a quotation. I make no comment upon it, except to say that this experience is by no means unique. It is the duty of the elders to do all they can to create and maintain the atmosphere of worship, not only on a Communion Sunday, but every Sunday.

The Elder's District

Perhaps the most important part of the elder's duty is the supervision of an elder's district. In his book on procedure, Cox writes:

The Kirk Session should arrange for the division of the congregation into convenient districts, and appoint one or more of its members to have special spiritual oversight of each district. Each elder ought to have a correct list of all those thus entrusted to his charge, members and adherents, and to report to the Kirk Session regarding them; it is his duty to visit the families in his district as their spiritual overseer, especially the aged and those in affliction, to care for the young, and to deal privately and tenderly with any who are neglecting public worship …

This, undoubtedly, is an important part of the elder's work and a great privilege. Sometimes when I am trying to persuade an individual to accept the office of eldership, I say, 'You will get an elder's district to look after, and get to know the people intimately. You will visit them and they will look forward to your visit—they will become your friends'. I remember once meeting an elder in an Edinburgh street. He said, 'I have had a very trying day in the office and I am now going to visit some of the people in my district. That will help me better than anything else'. His visit to these homes would not only be a blessing to them, it was also going to be a blessing for him.

It is always a pity when, for some reason or other, an elder posts the communion cards, delivers them like a postman. The best thing to do is to go *into* the house and chat with the people, get to know them, spend some time with them, talk to them about the Church—a tremendous amount of good can be done by the elder in this way. There may be children in the house who do not attend Sunday School—you could talk about that. Or there may be young people who could sing in the choir—you could pass their names on to the organist. There may be someone who wants to join the Church—you can tell the minister about them. Or there may be someone who is ill and the minister does not know about it. I always think that the best elder is the elder with the pastoral heart.

A Friendly Welcome

There is just one other duty I wish to emphasize. From time to time it is the duty of elders and office-bearers to stand at the church door and welcome those who enter. These are key individuals in the Church today. If we are going to bridge the

15

gulf between the Church and the non-churchgoing section of the community, there must be a friendly welcome, especially at the door of the church. How important it is that these office-bearers and elders should be friendly, welcoming men and women.

The days when certain pews belonged to certain people are, thankfully, gone. In those days it was important to welcome a stranger to one's pew. Stories survive of newcomers being asked to move out of a particular pew—hardly a welcoming attitude! Nowadays, with no pews 'reserved', it is still important for the regular churchgoer, as well as the elder, to extend a warm welcome to the visitor.

With church membership declining, perhaps it could be said that much of the future of the Church depends on winning outsiders. The Church today, if it is to be the true Church of Jesus Christ, must be a welcoming Church, with its door wide open to all who wish to enter and worship God.

A Visiting Minister

There is another visitor who should be welcomed to the church —a visiting minister. When your own minister is exchanging pulpits with another minister, it is the duty of the Session Clerk or one of the elders to go round to the vestry and welcome him or her. At the close of the service it is a friendly gesture for some of the elders to convey thanks on behalf of the church. It is a desolating experience for a minister to conduct a service or preach the gospel, and not one single person acknowledges the fact. If the minister has not done well, and you don't feel any great urge to go and say thanks, that is all the more reason why you should go. A friendly shake of the hand will help the minister do better next time. A word of encouragement is something we all need, ministers and office-bearers alike.

Spiritual Resources

When we think of the varied duties of the eldership and all that is involved in this spiritual office, we might well ask 'Who can manage *all* these things?' We cannot sit behind the communion table, in the very place of our Lord himself, without a sense of awe and unworthiness which only grows with the years. Not one of us can carry the symbols of Christ's Body and Blood to the people without realizing what we bear, and how unequal any of us are to the bearing of them.

But we must remember not only the service to which Christ calls us, we must also keep in mind the terms of the call: 'You did not choose me: I chose you' (John 15:16). It is Christ who has chosen us; and because Christ has chosen us we can count upon him to give us all the strength we need for our task. When we are doing God's work, we are never alone.

In the Old Testament story, Moses, hesitant and slow of speech, asked why he should be chosen to go to Pharaoh and lead out God's people. He raised one objection after another (almost as many objections as most people raise when asked to accept the eldership). But God brushed aside all his objections with the magnificent promise, 'I will be with you'; and he prefaced it with the word 'certainly'. There was no doubt about it; Moses could depend on it absolutely.

When Christ chooses one of us and calls us into his service, we can count upon Christ to provide all the help we need. Sometimes we may prove unworthy of our high calling and do things that bring discredit on the Church; but if we keep in touch with Christ, there is always the possibility of a new start. That is the great hope of the gospel: however badly we have done in the past, it is always possible to start again—tomorrow is a new day.

Part II

The Elder's Devotional Life

THE eldership is a spiritual office and only someone who has something of the Spirit of God within can fill it in any worthy way. Unspiritual men or women in the Session lower the spiritual temperature of the Church and destroy its power. That is why the devotional life of the elder is of supreme importance.

When we consider our devotional life it is always a good thing to have an ideal before us. Let us think of some of the great experts in the devotional life of the soul—like Paul, Augustine, Francis of Assisi, Thomas à Kempis, Martin Luther, John Wesley, John Calvin. These are the classic cases; but are there any features of the spiritual life of these men common to them all? A careful examination of their lives reveals one or two things.

Certainty of Religion

First of all, we notice that all these men possessed a wonderful certainty. When a man (or woman) finds God and gives himself to Christ, when he prays and reads his Bible every day, when he lives in fellowship with God and allows God to guide him, he achieves a wonderful spiritual independence. His feet are standing on a rock. He acquires an inner conviction that nothing can shake. Doubts and fears have no power to unsettle him; nor is he afraid of what other people might say. Nothing can daunt him. He is not afraid of misfortune or sorrow or suffering; even the passing of the years leaves him unafraid—for he knows that though the outward man perish, the inward man is renewed day by day. Like the Apostle Paul, he can say, 'that neither death, nor life ... nor things present, nor things to come, nor height, nor depth, nor any other creature, shall be able to separate us from the love of God which is in Christ Jesus our Lord'.

Singleness of Purpose

Second, such men are always dominated by a single purpose. Like the needle of a compass they always point in the same direction. Sometimes the needle may quiver, but it always comes back to the north. In the same way these souls may waver at times, but they always come back to Christ. Christ is the centre and source of their life. That is why, though they possess such a wonderful certainty, truly religious people never make others feel inferior. They know that the strength on which they are living is not drawn from their own resources, but from the everlasting springs of God.

Again, such people never need to speak about their religion or force it upon others, they never need to give any kind of personal testimony. Some do of course—and in the Christian life there is a place for such testimony—but it is not really necessary. They are like a mirror reflecting the light. Other people see it and are attracted by it, and sometimes they are compelled to ask, 'What must I do to be saved?'

Inner Peace

Third, such men have not only certainty and fixity of purpose, they have also an inner harmony which the New Testament calls *salvation*. They are at peace with God. They are at peace with their fellows. They are at peace with themselves. They have entered on a higher quality of life which is entirely different from every other form of human activity.

Contrast for a moment the religious experience with other forms of human activity. Think of scientific research. Think of the labour and work of our scientists, seeking a secret which often eludes them. Think of all this research and labour going on in our laboratories today, and then open your New Testament and there you will read the words of the Apostle Paul, 'I know whom I have believed, and am persuaded that he is able to keep that which I have committed unto him against that day'. The Apostle has found, he has achieved, he has arrived.

Or think of our social activity. Think of the various efforts that are being made to bring peace to the nations and create a sense of brotherhood; then go into a church, and in the worship of a Christian church you will find brotherhood achieved: rich and poor, high and low, learned and unlearned, meeting on a common level in the sight of God.

Or think of the moral struggle that never seems to end: the struggle with temptation, with pride and jealousy and passion. Then turn to the gospel and there you will hear Jesus saying, 'Be perfect as your Father in heaven is perfect'. Truly the religious experience is entirely different from every other form of human activity. It is a higher quality of life which the New Testament calls *eternal*.

These are the main features of the religious experience—certainty, fixity of purpose, interior peace, peace of mind, a sense of brotherhood, and peace of heart. When we analyze the religious experience in this way and realize what is involved in it, and what it can do for us, the question that must be in all our hearts is, 'How can we get this for ourselves?' There are various ways of answering that question, but perhaps the best way is to point to the evangelical means of grace which God has put at our disposal—*ie* prayer, Bible reading, public worship, self-discipline. There is no better way of deepening our devotional life than by making use of these evangelical means of grace.

The Means of Grace

First of all there is prayer. Every elder, like every minister, must have times of prayer; private and daily prayer. It is a great thing to have set times, and to bring some method into our prayer life. In the Old Testament story we are told that Daniel prayed three times a day. He had his place of prayer and fixed hours. There was nothing haphazard about his prayer life. It was ordered and disciplined. Morning, noon and night he knelt at his open window and had his time of quiet fellowship with God. I should like to commend Daniel's example and urge the necessity for method and habit in our prayer life.

Daniel prayed three times a day—morning, noon and night. It is not so easy to pray at noon as it is in the morning and evening. In the morning a new day has dawned. The sun is shining in at our window. The new day brings new opportunities for service, and we feel the need for God's help and guidance. So also in the evening, when darkness falls on the earth and the stars come into the sky, and the sense of eternity is all about us. What is more natural than to kneel down and thank God for the day that has gone and ask his forgiveness for any mistakes we have made?

It is not so easy to pray when we are busy in the shop or the office or the factory. There is nothing conducive to prayer there; and yet that is the time when we are most likely to forget God and when we most need to pray. To pray at noon we do not need to kneel, or even find seclusion. We can simply breathe a prayer to God in the shop or office or on the street, and who can tell what blessings these prayers may bring into our lives?

Bible Study

Second, there is Bible reading—daily, systematic reading of the Bible. It is not possible for any of us to have a vital Christian life if we do not know our Bible. It is sometimes said that the Bible is an easy book to read, and that is true of parts of it—the Psalms in the Old Testament, or the Gospel according to John in the New Testament, for example—but there are other parts of the Bible that are not so easy to read. We need to know the background, we need an explanation.

There is now a wide range of Bible study guides available. One of the most popular is the late Professor William Barclay's *Daily Study Bible* series which covers the entire New Testament in seventeen volumes. Published by The Saint Andrew Press, each volume includes the biblical text, divided into daily portions, along with a commentary on each day's reading, as well as helpful introductory material. With the help of study notes like these, office-bearers all over the country have started reading their Bibles again, discovering what a wonderful book the Bible really is.

It is a good thing in every church to have a Bible study group. Ministers sometimes hesitate about starting these groups, but wherever they exist, there is a wonderful response. All sorts of people come—the most unexpected people. Group study of the Bible is of great value because we can get something through the group that we cannot get alone. 'Where two or three are gathered together in my name, there am I in the midst of them' (Matthew 18:20).

Public Worship

Third, there is public worship. The presence of the elder in church, morning and evening, greatly encourages fellow worshippers. This is also a means of deepening the elder's own devotional life. How can the Christian life can be enriched without the fellowship of the Church and the public worship of God.

Some time ago one of our national newspapers conducted a religious poll of its many readers. The first question asked was, 'Is there a God?' The majority answered 'Yes'. So it would seem that there are very few agnostics and atheists in our country. The next question was, 'Can you be a Christian without going to church?' The majority answered 'Yes'. There is evidently a widespread impression among the people of our country that you can be a Christian whether you go to church or not. But that is very shallow and superficial thinking. Silence the church bells, close the church doors, shut down public worship, and Christianity as we know it would very soon disappear from Scotland. We need to gather week by week for the public worship of God if we are going to maintain and strengthen our spiritual life.

Self-Discipline

Then, last of all, there is self-discipline. That is also a means of bringing grace and control into our life. You may admire the self-controlled person who is poised, and not given to quick anger when something of a disturbing nature occurs; or who does not lose self-control when frustrated and disappointed. You may think that you have no power over yourself or over the way in which you react to conditions and situations in your life; but you do have this power. God has endowed you with qualities of mind and heart whereby you can develop the self-control and poise you admire in others.

It means effort. It means self-discipline. It means prayer, and it also means helping God to answer our prayers. There is an old saying, 'When you pray move your feet'—that is, do something to help God to answer your prayer. In the Lord's Prayer we use the petition, 'Lead us not into temptation'. But often we make no effort to keep out of temptation's way. It is frequently the reverse. We deliberately go where we know temptation is awaiting us; and when we fall we are inclined to put the blame on God. To me it seems a sheer waste of time to pray to God to keep us out of temptation if we head deliberately towards places where we know we will be tempted. We have to help God to answer our prayer by putting a discipline on ourselves. As Paul says, we have to stand by our prayer, 'praying always with all prayer and supplication in the Spirit, and watching thereunto with all perseverance' (Ephesians 6:18).

These are the various means that God has put at our disposal for the deepening and enriching of our devotional life. Any office-bearer who deliberately neglects these means of grace not only cuts him or herself off from the fellowship of God but destroys any usefulness in the Church; the eldership is, after all, a spiritual office; only someone who is touched with the Spirit of God can fill it in a worthy way. Unspiritual individuals in the Session always weaken the witness of a Christian Church and may bring discredit on the congregation.

Part III

The Elder in Person

Quartus the Brother (Romans 16:23)

AT the Battle of Trafalgar, Lord Nelson referred to his captains as 'one united band of brothers'. That was the secret of the great victory. Every Kirk Session, every Deacons' Court, every Board of Management, ought to be one united band of *brothers*. (Naturally this term is extended to include our *sisters* in the eldership as well.) In the Church of Christ there is room for men and women of different gifts and talents. One may have the gift of leadership and can express thoughts in stirring words. Another may have the gift of administration and can look after the organization of the Church. Another may have the gift of finance and at the end of the year can draw up a balance sheet. But whatever our gifts or talents, there is one quality that each of us must strive to possess—the quality of *brotherliness*.

The Church of Corinth was fortunate in this respect, for among the office-bearers there was a brotherly man called Quartus. What kind of man was he? We are not told very much about him but there are one or two things we can infer.

Not a distinguished Man

First, he was not a man of any conspicuous gift or St Paul would have said something about it; for the Apostle, when he mentioned any of his friends, usually added a descriptive phrase about their gifts and achievements. Timothy was his fellow-worker, Lucius and Jason were his kinsfolk, Erastus was the treasurer of the city; but there was nothing special said about Quartus. He had no outstanding gift. He occupied no great place in the city. Outside the little Christian community, perhaps nobody had even heard of him. He was not a leader. He was not a platform man. He was just a private in the army. He had no shoulder straps or decorations. He was the one-talent man of Christ's parable—but he, Quartus, did not bury his talent.

Further, he was not a man of wealth or social position. 'Not many wise men after the flesh, nor many mighty, not many noble were called' in the Church of Corinth. The Church in that city was mostly composed of slaves. There was an occasional man like Gaius, a man of means sufficient to enable him to act as host to Paul and to the whole Church; and there was an occasional Erastus, a man who held office in the local government of the city. Quartus, however, was just a specimen of things foolish and weak and base, from whose ranks the members of the Church at Corinth were mostly recruited. Quartus was one of the rank and file, one of the common, undistinguished multitude.

But although one-talented, he did not bury his talent in the earth like the man in Christ's parable. He ventured to use it. What he had he gave, becoming one of the most beloved, useful members of the Church of Corinth; even Paul associates him with himself in the despatch of his letter to the Romans. Thus he conferred on this one-talent man immortal fame. Wherever the gospel is preached, men shall hear of Quartus the brother.

The Friendly Man

What was the talent that Quartus used so faithfully? It is suggested by the words of description which the Apostle Paul appends to his name. He calls him Quartus *the brother.* That was the gift that Quartus possessed—brotherliness. He was a kind, genial man with the gift of befriending people. He had a genius for friendship. He could give people in trouble new courage and hope. That was the gift he laid at the feet of Christ, his contribution to the well-being of the Church at Corinth. He was Quartus the brother. And the Church at Corinth had no more useful member than Quartus. He was not so well-off as Gaius, he was not so influential as Erastus; but perhaps he did more for the happiness and peace of the congregation than either of these men.

The Church at Corinth was a difficult Church. It was split up into sects and parties. Some supported Paul, others Apollos, others Cephas. There was a great deal of careless talk and endless criticism, and whenever the spirit of criticism gets into a Kirk Session or a Deacons' Court it has a very negative influence. It can wreck everything. I can well imagine that the Church at Corinth might have been broken up altogether had it not been for Quartus. He created a friendly atmosphere. He was a reconciling spirit. When he heard an office-bearer being criticized, he always had something good to say for him. He did everything in his power to secure the peace and harmony of the congregation, putting himself a great deal of trouble and inconvenience. He was Quartus the brother.

By helping to maintain peace and harmony, Quartus was of service to the whole congregation; but there were two classes to whom he was especially helpful. First of all, to those in trouble or distress, when sorrow or bereavement, for instance, darkened a home. Quartus was always there with his sympathy and help. He was not particularly eloquent at expressing his feeling; but the warm grasp of his hand brought comfort to many a troubled soul. And, second, when anyone broke with the pagan religion and proclaimed faith in Christ by joining the Church, Quartus made a special point of befriending that person. It was not easy to confess Christ in those days. It meant suffering and persecution. It meant the loss of home and kin and friends; and Quartus tried to make good that loss. He did his best to make the new converts feel that although they had lost one family, they had gained another. He was Quartus the brother.

The Need of the Hour

I have brought this man before you because I feel that Quartus the brother is the need of the hour. We cannot shut our eyes to the fact that the Church has entered a new period of persecution and frustration; but however critical the situation there is no grounds for despair and despondency. On the other hand, there is much to cheer and encourage us. All over the country we find a new urge towards Christian unity. Just as at one time there was a tendency to splinter, today there is a tendency to unite. We find Churches of all denominations—Presbyterian, Episcopal, Congregational, Baptist, Methodist—working together, presenting a united front to the forces of evil. That is something very significant in Scotland. Again, there is a growing demand for reality in worship and doctrine. Congregations may not be as large as they once were, but certainly there is a new reality in our services. Preaching is more real, and the devotional part of the services is more in touch with life in our time. People are coming to realize that a church service where you have hearty congregational singing, and preaching that is in touch with the Bible and life, can be a great help and inspiration to us all.

Again, there is an increasing awareness that evangelism can no longer be the hobby of a few enthusiasts, but must more and more become the obligation of the whole Church and of every member of the Church. Today all Christians stand in the front line of the battle and every elder must be an evangelist, seeking to win others for Christ and his Church; and in this work of evangelism none can play a more important part than Quartus the brother. We need Quartus the brother in all our churches. We need him in the Kirk Session; we need him in the Deacons' Court; we need him on the Board of Management; we need him in the pew; we need him standing in the vestibule giving a welcome to strangers.

Quartus the brother, the man who creates a friendly atmosphere in the church, who welcomes strangers, who takes a real interest in his fellow members and has a word of greeting for all: will anyone deny that Quartus the brother is the need of the hour? And remember it does not require outstanding gifts. It just needs a big loving heart. What a difference it would make to all our churches, if only we had more men like Quartus.

Dr J D Jones, who in his day was a great leader, a brotherly man, was fond of telling a story about a tombstone which he found in a little graveyard in the West of England. At the foot of the stone were engraved the words, '*Quartus the brother*'. He made enquiries and discovered that the stone marked the grave of a man who was deeply devoted to the Church and did everything he could in his own quiet brotherly way to help the Church and his fellow-members. Whenever there was any dissension or any trouble, he tried to pour oil on the troubled waters. When he died this was the phrase he wished to have engraved on his tombstone: *'Quartus the brother'*.

This man's humility is seen in his request. He wanted no mention made of his gifts, or his place in the Church, or his splendid service. He wanted to be remembered simply as one who had tried to be a brother. Really, what higher title could any man have? Gifts of leadership and organization may not be ours, but we can all become like Quartus the brother. That is something within the reach of us all. Our biography may never be written. Our name may never appear in any honours list; but our life will not have been in vain if, when God calls us to come, the men among whom we have lived, and whose burdens we have helped to bear, shall inscribe on our tombstone the words, *'Quartus the brother'*.